G000021012

T̶O̶O̶L̶S̶

for

Anxiety

Toolkit
for
Anxiety

AN INTRODUCTION

Easy to use tools and techniques to help you cope with your anxiety, anytime, anywhere.

Annabel Marriott

THE CHOIR PRESS

Copyright © 2020 Annabel Marriot

All rights reserved. No part of this publication may be reproduced or transmitted in any form or by any means, electronic or mechanical including photocopying, recording or any information storage or retrieval system, without prior permission in writing from the publishers.

The right of Annabel Marriot to be identified as the author of this work has been asserted by her in accordance with the Copyright, Designs and Patents Act 1988

First published in the United Kingdom in 2020 by The Choir Press

ISBN 978-1-78963-143-2

Disclaimer

This book is not intended to act as a substitute for professional treatment. If you are experiencing severe, debilitating anxiety that is adversely affecting you, please seek professional help as soon as you can.

Author's Note

Anxiety is an unpleasant part of everyday life and can affect us in a myriad of ways. But the first thing to understand is that it is completely natural and the power to overcome it lies within you.

However, if you are experiencing anxiety, know that you are not alone.

It is my hope that within these pages, you will find some tools and techniques that work for you. **Whoever** you are and **wherever** you are on your journey right now, these techniques are simple to learn and easy to apply. We can do much to improve our personal wellbeing through our own self-care and awareness of what helps us to feel better; not tomorrow, next week, next month or next year but at this very moment: right here, right now.

This is a little book for your back pocket, a little book to take anywhere. Use it as a starting point. Like a toolkit, it's designed to be portable. Remember, you are an expert on yourself and no one size fits all. When you find a tool that works for you, it is important to repeat it on a regular basis so that it becomes a familiar part of your day-to-day routine. Like a true best friend, it won't let you down in times of trouble.

Contents

Life's challenges are not supposed to paralyse you, they're supposed to help you discover who you are.

Bernice Johnson Reagon –
musician, author and social activist

Introduction

As the founder of analytical psychology, Carl Jung put it, *'We cannot change anything unless we accept it.'*

This is certainly the case with anxiety. Perhaps you've tried to ignore it up until now. It may surprise you to learn that the most important step is to **accept your anxiety. It's OK to do so.** This may seem like an alien concept but once you accept uncomfortable feelings and realise they are a part of everyday life, the sooner you can begin to get rid of them.

So what's happening?

The **amygdala** is a small almond-shaped organ. It is the ancient part of the brain and is responsible for our 'fight or flight' response. Thousands of years ago it would alert us to the very real dangers of living in the wild, but nowadays, thankfully, most of us don't have to worry about encountering a ferocious lion before breakfast!

Adrenaline and cortisol flood the body when our 'emotional brain' senses danger. Our heart rate is increased and oxygen is sent to our limbs to enable us to fight or fly. Believe it or not, the brain can't actually distinguish the difference between a real danger and an imagined danger, so it will react in the same way. That's why thinking of the things you fear leads to unease and discomfort, because your brain is telling you to take action.

The amygdala alerts us to the fact that we need to do something to be safe and therefore serves a very useful purpose when we are in real danger. Think of it as your internal warning system.

Anxiety is not something we have; it's something we do. It's an emotional response to a situation that is experienced as threatening.

> When you are anxious, the thoughts you have are
> the product of a brain that
> has changed to
> accommodate anxiety.

Dr Patrick Partington – senior lecturer and research fellow in health psychology, Southampton University

If you think of something specific that causes you anxiety and you really give it some attention, you may get a familiar sensation in your body. Feeling a tightness across your chest or a knot in your stomach? The same old images and thoughts might re-emerge. This is because you are defaulting to the well-trodden pathways that have become embedded in your subconscious mind.

The great news is that you can re-wire your brain to feel differently. Yes. Our brain can actually re-wire itself! This is due to something called neuroplasticity.

Every time we learn something new, we create fresh neural connections. Just knowing this can make us feel a whole lot better as we come to see that the ability to alter the way we think, feel and behave is possible.

So, let's begin with some ancient wisdom. When we make our entrance into the world, it's the very first thing we do ... **BREATHE.**

The Power of Breath

> Breathing is the pace you set
> your life at; it's the rhythm
> of the song of you.

Matt Haig – author and journalist

Deep breathing helps to calm an overactive nervous system. It can have a profound effect on both your mental and physical wellbeing and is not to be underestimated. Research has shown that there is a neural circuit in the brainstem known as the brain's 'breathing pacemaker'. If we are breathing quickly and erratically, activity increases, whereas if we are breathing in a slow, controlled manner, the activity in the circuit is lowered.

When we are feeling anxious we need to engage the **parasympathetic nervous system,** and focused breathing techniques engage this 'relax and renew response'. The simple act of breathing deeply in and slowly breathing out has the effect of bringing the heart rate down and reducing blood pressure.

If you are somebody who suffers from anxiety from the moment you wake up in the morning, breathing deeply can be a powerful way to create some calm before the business of the day begins.

There are hundreds of different breathing techniques. **Here are three that you may find helpful:**

The Relaxing Breath

Apply this breathing to instantly relax.

Gently place your hand over your abdomen.

Close your eyes.

Breathe in for five counts – feel your abdomen swell out.

Breathe out for seven counts – simply imagine the word 'RELAX' as you breath out.

Feel your abdomen reduce and flatten gently towards your spine.

The Calming Breath

Tell yourself you are doing a good job, whether you believe it or not.

Breathe in slowly through the nose and acknowledge how you are feeling.

Allow yourself to be OK to feel this way.

Breathe out more slowly through the mouth, projecting your breath over a half closed throat Think Darth Vader!

The 4-7-8 Breath

This works wonders for calming an over-stimulated nervous system.

Take a slow, deep breath in through the nose counting to four.

Hold for seven.

Breathe out through the mouth for eight.

Go deeper into those sensations of fear and embrace them. Once you have acknowledged they are there, they will begin to lose their power over you.

Experiment by doing any of these breathing exercises for just fifteen minutes a day to benefit from the hugely therapeutic effect. You might like to do short one or two-minute sessions, as the effect is cumulative.

If, at any time, you find you are really stuck and feel a wave of panic or become overwhelmed, just breathe deeply and focus upon something positive. This could be a cherished memory of a person, place or thing. It could be imagined. What matters is that you give it your full attention. Immerse yourself in the present moment. Take control. Start to direct the movies in your head.

The Power of Pattern Interrupt

"The way that we break habits in the brain is by interrupting the pattern and forcing the brain out of that loop and into something else."

Melissa Tiers – founder of the Center for Integrative Hypnosis, New York

These straightforward practical exercises are designed to interrupt your pattern of anxiety. Remember, when we 'do' anxiety we keep taking the old familiar pathway, which means we feel those same bodily sensations and we probably behave in the same way too – the fight or flight response. Furthermore, when we get anxious we tend to be using the right hemisphere of our brain only. Our focus is extremely narrow as we fixate upon the situation, person or 'thing'. We want to employ both sides of our brain to interrupt the pattern of fear.

These techniques can enable you to move into a less anxious state where you can feel calmer and more in control. As with all of these tools, the more often you use them, the better you will be able to feel and cope in any given situation.

You may be surprised; these can stop anxiety in its tracks in just a minute or two.

Bilateral Stimulation

Pause for a moment and think about the thing you want to change. How intense is your feeling of discomfort? Give it a number from one to ten, with ten being the most intense.

Think about how you want to feel instead. Focus on that.

Now take any object that you can pass from one hand to the other. It can be a bunch of keys, a tennis ball, a water bottle, anything that you can pass from one side to the other. Just make sure you are crossing the middle line of your body. Do this a few times until you notice that the intensity of feeling has dropped. Check in with yourself. What number are you at now? Keep going until you feel better.

You can use this virtually any time any place, although this technique will be at its most effective when you are actually 'doing' your anxiety.

The Butterfly Hug

This wonderful technique was developed by practitioner Lucina Artigas and is widely used by therapists to help reduce anxiety and trauma. It is empowering and calming and helps you to focus on the present moment.

Sitting down in a comfortable position, with your hands on your thighs, take a few deep breaths: in through the nose, out through the mouth. Think about what is troubling you. Notice how agitated you feel. You can give it a number from one to ten, with ten being the most disturbing.

Begin by placing your right hand on your left upper arm and your left hand on your right upper arm, or can you place your hands on your chest and link your thumbs together.

You can keep your eyes gently closed or you can look toward the tip of your nose.

Keep your hands and fingers pointed upwards, towards the chin.

Keeping your wrists on your chest, slowly alternate the movement of your hands, tapping gently like the flapping wings of a butterfly.

Let your hands move freely, gently tapping up and down. Observe your thoughts and feelings. Notice any physical sensations. What's coming up for you?

Continue to breathe slowly and deeply.

Let your hands rest. Notice what is going through your mind; again, become aware of any physical sensations. Try not to push your thoughts away, or have any judgment. Just be aware and accept. Has anything shifted? Are you at the same number you started with, or has the intensity lessened at all? As long as you are reducing the level, you know you are going in the right direction.

Spend a few minutes here.

If further uncomfortable thoughts and feelings arise, continue to breathe slowly and deeply. Repeat this butterfly hug if helpful, until you feel the negative emotions have released.

You may find it easier to watch a video talking you through this technique. See psychologist

Rebecca Sophia Strong's demonstration on YouTube:

'Butterfly Hug for Finding Calm in Chaotic Times'.

The methods above are forms of **bilateral stimulation**. Activity flows through both hemispheres of the brain, helping to disperse those anxious feelings.

Now in order to turn the volume down on what can be a constant internal dialogue, use your **peripheral vision.** This engages your parasympathetic nervous system (the relaxation response). Without the ongoing loop of negative self-talk, it's a lot harder for the anxiety to take a hold.

Focus upon a point in front of you and then start to go into peripheral vision without moving your eyes. Expand your awareness to your environment and what is at the edge of your field of vision. If you are inside, expand your awareness to the walls, the windows, the floor. Keep widening your vision. Be aware that you are broadening out from that central focus. Imagine you can see the space around you expanding. Notice what you see and hear. Enjoy being there. Your breathing will slow down and your body will begin to relax. Now gently return to your first point of focus. Repeat two or three times until you feel calmer.

Emotional Freedom Technique (EFT) or tapping as it is widely referred to, is a brief technique that is easy to learn. You don't need to be a master practitioner to get rapid results. You can think of it as being like acupuncture without the needles.

You tap with your fingertips on a series of meridian end points on your face and body. This sends a calming signal to your brain, telling it you're safe.

Begin by taking a deep breath in through the nose and breathing out through the mouth. Note any tension in your body. Rate the intensity of the emotion you are feeling by giving it a number from one to ten with one being the least intense and ten being the most.

State the problem out loud in a few words and be as specific as you can.

Use a short self-acceptance statement such as 'Even though I'm feeling really anxious/stressed/upset (whatever you are feeling), I love and accept myself.' Or if this is too hard right now, try 'I accept how I'm feeling.'

Use your second and third fingers to tap firmly but not harshly on the meridian points listed whilst repeating the set-up statement. You can use one hand or two. Whatever feels most comfortable.

Once you have repeated the setup statement three times on the karate chop point, you can simply use a reminder phrase such as 'all this anxiety'.

Repeat the process three or four times until your intensity level has dropped. It may only be a little to begin with. Keep tapping and see what happens.

Karate chop – bottom side of the wrist.

Eyebrow point – where the eyebrow meets the nose.

Side of the eye.

Under the eye.

Under the nose.

Between the lower lip and the chin.

Collarbone.

Under the armpit.

Top of the head – towards the back.

It may be easier to watch a video in the first instance to help you learn the tapping points.

Once you've learned the basic sequence and completed a few rounds of tapping, you'll have a tool that you can use rapidly and regularly in your daily life.

For everything you need to get you started, see: **www.thetappingsolution.com**

The Power of Imagination

"Imagination is everything. It is the preview of life's coming attractions."

Albert Einstein

Our imagination is one of the most powerful tools we have. This is why we may experience physical sensations and mental angst when we simply imagine an anxiety-provoking event. The amygdala is being fired in the same way as it would if this event were actually happening. So if you think about and rehearse a scenario where you see yourself as confident, positive and in control, when it comes to the real situation your brain will be ready and will not automatically revert to your old way of thinking, feeling and behaving. The more you rehearse the event with a positive mindset, the stronger the impact will be on the subconscious. Rehearse, rehearse, rehearse. Employ as many senses as you can. Eventually you will start to feel it. Imagination opens up new possibilities and provides us with options on how to respond when we encounter a problem.

Serotonin affects our mood in a positive way and is often referred to as 'the feelgood chemical'. You can harness your imagination to think about positive things in the same way as you use it to think about the negatives. So why not get a healthy dose of serotonin in its most natural form?

What follows is a short, guided visualisation. At some point, you might like to record yourself so that you can play it whenever you need to. Alternatively, you may just begin to get familiar with it so that you can take your eyes off the page and relax into it.

Near the end of the visualisation, we set an 'anchor' for positive feelings. It might help you to think of an anchor as something that connects our conscious awareness to a memory, a person or an emotion. We set up anchors all the time without realising it. Remember that old song that takes you back to a specific time in your life? Or a particular smell that transports you in an instant to the memory of a person or a place? That's because our brain is making an association to something in the past. When we want to anchor a positive feeling, we can create them ourselves. They are at their most effective when combined with the senses and can have a profound effect when we implement them in times of stress.

Just get yourself comfortable and we'll begin . . .

You can use your imagination now to help your mind become relaxed. You can allow your subconscious to think of the safest and most relaxing place you can imagine . . . perhaps it's a place that you've been to . . . or a place that you'd like to go . . . or just somewhere in your imagination where you are able to relax deeply.

Take a moment to enjoy being there now, in the safest, most relaxing place that you can imagine . . . noticing all the things that make it so good

. . . all the things you can see around you . . . and you can use your imagination now to make the colours brighter and better . . . noticing the sounds you can hear . . . or perhaps it's the quiet that you enjoy . . . perhaps there's a taste, or a smell, that reminds you of this place . . . and you can notice all of the sensations in your body that let you know that you are safe and secure . . . calm and relaxed . . . continuing to notice all the things . . . the sights . . . the sounds . . . everything that reminds you of those feelings inside you . . . peaceful . . . comfortable . . . relaxed . . . just noticing them now . . . just enjoying being in that place . . .

And now . . . taking a deep breath in as you squeeze one of your wrists tightly and hold your breath for one, two, three seconds and as you slowly breathe out, just say the words 'safe and secure' to yourself in your own mind as you sink deeper into these relaxed and confident feelings . . .

Taking a deep breath in . . . squeeze your wrist tightly, now hold your breath for one . . . two . . . three seconds . . . and now slowly breathe out, as you say the words 'safe and secure' quietly in your own mind . . .

And you can sink even deeper into these feelings that you have now . . . as you continue to enjoy being in your safe and relaxing place.

Stay here for at least five minutes. Gently bring yourself back to the present, and as you do so, become aware of the different ways in which life can be better for you.

You have now set a confidence anchor that is wrapped up with feelings of safety and security. Any time you want to change the way you feel, you can do so easily just by firing your anchor and allowing all of those positive sensations to come flooding back, reminding yourself that you're in control of how you feel.

If you would like to listen to the audio, please go to: **www.toolkitforanxiety.com**

The Power of Reshaping your Thoughts

You cannot always control what goes on outside. But you can always control what goes on inside.

Wayne Dyer – psychologist, author and motivational speaker

The world can be a scary place and it is not difficult to find things to worry about. But a lot of these are most likely out of our control. As an Olympian rower once stated in a television interview, he could only affect that which was inside his boat. These were things he had personal control over: eating the right diet, getting enough sleep and carrying out the proper training. Everything else, such as how his competitors were performing and the weather conditions were 'outside of his boat' and he would not let them affect him.

Perhaps you can locate some of the things that are troubling you and identify whether they are 'inside' or 'outside' of your 'boat'. You may find it useful to make a list. If outside, then aim to accept that they can't be changed and focus on the things that **are** within your control instead.

Attempting to suppress a thought can be like trying to push a beach ball under the water. It just keeps popping up and the harder we try the more difficult it becomes to stop it popping up.

Imagine if you had lots of these balls and you had to keep them all under control beneath the surface of the water. It would be impossible, but that's often what we try to do. The solution is simple; stop trying to control the balls. They aren't going to stay under the water so just allow them to float around you.

You might not get rid of them completely but as you learn to live with them they will become less bothersome. Remember, thoughts are just thoughts. Accept them and direct your attention to where it is of better use.

Cognitive Behavioural Therapy (CBT as it is commonly known) deals with the way we think. Our thoughts affect the way we feel, and the way we feel affects how we behave. It is one of the most widely used and comprehensively researched forms of therapy for anxiety. Its aim is to help you find a more positive way of thinking and to challenge any unhelpful underlying assumptions you may have about yourself or others.

CBT can enable you to develop strategies to empower you to face your anxieties rather than run away from them.

So next time you feel the panic rising, aim to tune into what's going on in your mind. What are you telling yourself about the situation, person or event? What images are you conjuring up? Write these down if you can. It's important to acknowledge these thoughts rather than attempting to suppress them as just like the beach balls, they will keep re-surfacing no matter how hard you try to suppress them.

When you have a negative or disturbing thought, are you able to reshape it into something more positive? Even if it's a tiny adjustment, it may be very helpful. If you are nervous about giving a presentation, for example, you might be telling yourself 'I can't stand this, everyone's looking at me'. Could you tweak this to something like: 'This isn't very comfortable and I'm not enjoying it but I'm able to get through this'? Whatever you are telling yourself, you need to be able to believe these new thoughts, so they must be authentic.

If you would like to learn more about how your thinking affects your emotions and behaviour, you might explore CBT and Rational Emotive Behavioural Therapy (REBT). There is plenty of material available on both and you can search for accredited practitioners online.

The Power of Nature

"We are all familiar with the feelings of relaxation and switching off which comes from a walk in the countryside and now we have evidence from the brain and the body which helps us understand the effect."

Cassandra Gould van Praag, PhD –
neuroscientist and researcher in psychiatry

Being connected to the natural world helps cultivate inner tranquillity and positivity. Spending time in nature, be it with trees, mountains, rivers or at the beach, can help you to gain perspective and draw you out of your overwhelmed internal world. Research also suggests that time spent in the great outdoors can work wonders for our immune system.

Taking a twenty-minute stroll in a green space, anywhere with trees and plants – a recreation ground, a wood or a garden – helps distract you from everyday stresses. Blood pressure drops and the heart rate decreases. It can help clear your mind when too much time is spent in front of screens and your energy has been sapped. You don't have to exercise vigorously to feel the mental and physical benefits.

If you struggle to spend time outdoors, start small and spend just five minutes a day in the open air. Look up at the sky, notice the trees. Aim to stay present. If your body is tense, notice where you are carrying this tension. Become an observer of your thoughts and physical sensations.

In an article for Inc.com, Richard Shuster, clinical psychologist and host of *The Daily Helping* podcast, stated that 'Staring at the ocean actually changes our brain waves' frequency and puts us into a mild meditative state.' Next time you are able to get to the seaside, breathe deeply and enjoy the feeling, knowing it's doing you a whole lot of good!

Planting a few of your own vegetables has a great feelgood factor. You can grow your own produce even if you have very limited outdoor space. Nothing beats watching your own seeds take root and prosper. You can start them off on a windowsill in a little bit of seed compost. Old egg boxes and plastic takeaway cartons are ideal for this. You can then transfer them to a few deep pots, a balcony or a window box. Get creative! Lettuce, tomatoes, courgettes and plenty of different varieties of herbs can easily be grown from seed.

If you'd rather start with more mature seedlings or plants, you can pick up a little pot of parsley or basil from your local greengrocer or supermarket. Why not grow your favourite flowers this way too? You'll probably want to divide the plants and re-pot them into larger containers or pop them straight into the ground. There is a wealth of information online to explore options for growing your own.

The addition of a few houseplants to your home or working environment can work wonders. Apart from increasing the oxygen levels, plants help 'cleanse the air' by removing indoor pollutants through their roots and leaves. They can help to alleviate stress and improve cognitive function besides being beautiful to look at.

The Power of Sound

"The sound of waves can help you achieve a meditative state, which is proven to heal and strengthen your brain ... These slow, whooshing noises are the sounds of non-threats, which is why they work to calm people; it's like they're saying: "Don't worry, don't worry, don't worry."

Orfeu Buxton – associate professor of biobehavioural health, Pennsylvania State University

Researchers seem to have pinpointed why sounds from nature are so powerful in calming the 'flight or fight' response. The vibrations change the connections in our brain and can affect our heart rate.

There are many soothing relaxation tracks available to listen to online that include the sound of rain falling, ocean waves, birdsong and music specifically composed to promote deeper sleep. The choice is yours!

Centerpointe Research have developed audio technology used by over two million people worldwide 'to create changes in the brain's electrical activity'. Research conducted by the Mt Sinai Medical Center and Menninger Clinic led to the introduction of Holosync audio technology. You can listen to a free demonstration to get a feel for it. All you need is the internet and a pair of headphones.

See: **www.centerpointe.com**

Listening to your favourite music can be a great comfort and provides you with the opportunity to relax and re-centre. Again, it's about personal choice and what works best for you. Five minutes of listening to a life-affirming piece of music can help set you up for the day: in the shower, in your car, through your headphones – whatever works for you. Perhaps you can create your own soundtrack that helps you feel more uplifted or grounded?

The Power of Eating Healthily

"There's something really empowering about making a conscious decision to start your day by doing something so nourishing and nurturing for yourself before you've made any other decisions; it really puts you on the right track to have a positive day."

Ella Woodward – bestselling food writer and entrepreneur

lemon

grapefruit

apple

orange

peach

It is widely accepted that consuming more fruit and vegetables can help improve your overall wellbeing. There are plenty of other ways to ensure you get the right amount of vitamins and nutrients too by adding foods that are known for their stress-busting qualities.

Aim to include plenty of dark green leafy vegetables in your diet such as broccoli, kale and spinach; they contain **magnesium** and **folate** which produce **dopamine**, the pleasure-inducing brain chemical that helps keep you calm. Magnesium is needed in order for the central nervous system to function properly. It can help promote a more restful night's sleep. This mineral can become depleted during periods of stress and so it's important to ensure you keep your levels topped up. **Bananas, molasses and cashew nuts** are also excellent sources of this mineral. Studies have shown that a lack of folate in the diet can lead to higher anxiety. An excellent source of folate can be found in asparagus as well as broccoli, citrus fruits and legumes. **B vitamins** are contained in a multitude of foods including green leafy vegetables and fish. **Vitamin B 6 is** needed for overall health and wellbeing. **B12** is essential for keeping your nervous system healthy and a lack of it can lead to mood imbalance and tiredness. You may want to take a good vitamin B complex supplement. If in doubt, consult your pharmacist or doctor.

Berries are full of antioxidants and phytonutrients which help to improve your body's response to stress. There's a reason why **blueberries** are given the superfood status! They're crammed with antioxidants and rich in **vitamin C.**

Selenium may help to reduce inflammation, which is thought to be heightened if you are prone to anxiety. Foods that contain **selenium** include **Brazil nuts, mushrooms and soya beans.**

Omega-3 is essential for brain health. The highest concentration can be found in **oily fish: salmon, sardines and smoked mackerel.** These are also an excellent source of **vitamin E,** which is linked to cognitive function and emotional wellbeing. **Seaweed** too provides a rich source, as does **hemp, flaxseed and chia seeds.** Try introducing some of these ingredients into your meals and the enjoyment of cooking something both delicious and nutritious may help alleviate any stress or anxiety you are feeling.

Often referred to as 'the good vitamin', or the 'sunshine vitamin', **vitamin D** is very important when it comes to anxiety and stress-related conditions. Our reserves built up during the summer can become depleted so it may be worth upping your intake, particularly in the winter months. You could take a regular dose of cod liver oil or, if you want a vegan alternative, you could try algae oil capsules instead. In order to optimise the body's ability to absorb this vitamin, you could add a generous amount of rosemary and sage to your cooking. Not only will these tasty herbs be doing you a whole lot of good, their addition will make your cooking go with a zing!

The Brain–Gut Connection

Clinical trials suggest the bacteria in our guts alters the activity in our brain. Indeed, the connection between brain and gut health has become widely accepted, so much so that the gut is now sometimes referred to as the 'Second Brain'.

Probiotics are the live bacteria which help to keep your gut healthy. Natural yogurt (not the sugary sweetened version) is one of the best sources. This can be dairy or non-dairy. Miso is also an excellent source. This is a fermented soya bean paste; a tasty addition to homemade soups. You can also take probiotics in tablet form and there are plenty of brands available from your local chemist, health food shop or online suppliers. Studies upon the effect of **Lactobacillus reuteri** in particular indicate a positive effect on easing anxiety.

If you find yourself getting agitated during the day, look at how much caffeine you are drinking, especially during the afternoon and evening. A cup or two of real coffee in the morning can be one of life's joys and shouldn't be a problem for most people. But overdoing the caffeine can make anxiety worse, so you might want to switch to decaffeinated or a herbal tea of your preferred taste such as chamomile, liquorice or lemon verbena. Those that contain valerian can also be very soothing. If you are pregnant, however, be aware that green tea contains caffeine and can reduce the absorption of folate.

When possible, replace white carbohydrates with wholegrain bread and rice. Lower the amount of ready meals or 'fast foods' you consume which can be high in salt and sugar and low in nutritional value. Avoid caffeinated sports drinks and unnecessary additives if you can and steer clear of processed sugar. Instead, stick to the natural sugars found in fruit. Try a teaspoon of honey in your tea instead of synthetic sweetener.

If you are a chocolate lover, read on! **There are antioxidants in cocoa** and organic dark chocolate contains unique natural substances that create a sense of euphoria. It also contains magnesium. Go for varieties that contain at least 70% cocoa. The amino acid, tryptophan, that is found in chocolate also happens to be the precursor to serotonin. Good news all round!

The Power of Community

There is plenty of evidence of co-operation among individuals of many species ... Birds call warnings to each other; the grooming of monkeys is reciprocal. The natural world confirms that we are stronger in community.

Jennifer Kavanagh – speaker, writer and founder of the Open Wing Trust

The need to belong, to be part of something greater than ourselves, is an inherent part of the human condition. Often we seek reassurance from others when we are uncertain. We look for groups of people with whom we can identify and share a common bond, whether that be a shared religious belief or playing for or supporting the same sports team. Put simply, community is about responding to each other's needs. Through connecting with others we learn more about kindness and compassion.

Feeling isolated and alone is not good for your wellbeing. If you spend a fair amount of time on your own, the chances are you get inside your own head too much. It's possible you metaphorically beat yourself up for feeling or acting in a particular way. Be kinder to yourself if you can. Remember, you are a work in progress.

Having a few good friends and a supportive family is going to help but not all of us are fortunate enough to have a support network like this.

In the UK, 'Social prescribing' is a relatively new government initiative introduced to help individuals struggling with loneliness. Doctors can now 'prescribe' a person to a link worker who can explore local activities alongside medication or as a standalone 'therapy' that can range from singing in a community choir to gardening clubs, walking, dancing and cooking. If you think this might help you, ask your doctor's surgery for details on what's going on in your locality.

Perhaps there is a self-help group in your vicinity? Being part of a supportive, non-judgmental network can be of enormous benefit. Sharing your experiences may help you to overcome some of your battles with anxiety and may well help others in the process as you are being courageous in sharing your feelings. There is no shame in admitting you need to offload. Sometimes simply being able to share what's on your mind is enough. The very fact that someone has taken the time to listen in a non-judgmental environment can be a huge relief in itself.

There may be local projects you can volunteer with. It could be worth looking at opportunities near you by going on volunteering websites.

If you enjoy being outdoors, the National Trust and the Woodland Trust are often looking for people to help in various capacities. Taking that first step can be challenging; the key is to find an activity that you enjoy doing.

At the Start of
Your Day

Aim to set your alarm ten to fifteen minutes earlier than usual or wake up naturally if you can. When you realise you do have the time to focus on your own wellbeing, real change can start to happen.

Beginning each morning with a ritual that includes deep breathing and gentle or more vigorous exercise can help to ensure your day gets off to the best possible start. This might include some yoga, a stretching routine and a five-minute meditation. Build it into your daily routine if you can and it will soon become a habit just like brushing your teeth or taking a shower. Maintaining a positive structure and routine that you and you alone have control over is the perfect way to start the day and will help you navigate any challenges you may face. Avoid switching on your mobile phone the minute you wake up so you are not immediately drawn into the noise of the outside world.

You may already keep a mood log in which you can express your thoughts and feelings on paper. Doing so allows you to self-monitor from day to day and from month to month and to observe any reoccurring negative patterns of thought. You will begin to identify more clearly what triggers your anxiety and what may help to calm it down. Start to give your brain and body the space to be more present to yourself and to those around you.

Smoothies are a great way to kick start your day and are an excellent way to increase your fruit and vegetable intake. Making and enjoying your own homemade nutrient-rich smoothies can be creative and fun! Frozen fruit can supplement fresh fruit and makes preparation quicker.

Experiment with whatever fruit and veg you like. You'll find plenty of ideas online to get your juices flowing! Eat a nutritious breakfast if you can. A handful of almonds and seeds, scrambled eggs or sugar-free muesli are all great foods to energise your mind and body first thing.

At the End of
Your Day

It can be all too easy to go to sleep looking at a screen and to wake up to one too. Do your best to avoid engaging with any technology within an hour before you go to bed and leave your mobile/laptop downstairs. Research suggests that the blue light from laptops and mobile phones can lead to sleep deprivation. Instead, make time for idleness and thinking.

How about keeping a **gratitude journal?** Write down **three things that you are grateful for. You can do this every day or on a weekly basis.** Some may seem inconsequential, but however small and seemingly insignificant, note them down. Doing this before bedtime is especially beneficial as it primes the mind to expect good things the next day. Whatever time you choose to do it, putting pen to paper and noting down what you are grateful for can help you to focus upon the positive and can distract you from dwelling upon the negative. However difficult life gets and however hard it may feel, there is always something to be grateful for.

Why not give it a go? You have nothing to lose and everything to gain.

Before turning in, there's a lot to be said for a nice warm bath. Light a few candles and turn off the lights. Add a handful of Epsom salts or a few drops of pure essential oils such as **lavender** and **geranium** in the water. See if you can let go physically and mentally. Make time for yourself. A few drops under your pillow can aid restful sleep whilst smelling rather lovely too.

Pure essential oils can be purchased from most health food shops and online at:
www.tisserand.com

Thank you for reading this book

If this little book helps just one person, I will be very happy. I hope it is you.

Keep an open mind if you can and continue to search for the tools and techniques that work for you.

I believe there is something out there for everyone.

I hope you never give in to your anxiety but work to find ways to banish it from your life.

Never give up on yourself. You are unique, you are powerful and you have all the resources you need within you.

I wish you the very best of luck and remember . . .

> We learn to fly not by becoming fearless but by the daily practice of courage.

Sam Keen – author, professor and philosopher

Time to Reflect

What do I want my life to look like?

What tools can I use to help me
get there?

THOUGHTS

DREAMS

NOTES

About the Author

Annabel Marriott is a teacher, trainer and clinical hypnotherapist specialising in anxiety, fears and phobias. She is registered with the General Hypnotherapy Council and is an approved therapist with Anxiety UK.

www.toolkitforanxiety.com

Acknowledgements

My heartfelt thanks go to Dr Patrick Partington for his inspiration and encouragement and for giving his permission for some of his techniques to be reproduced in this publication.

www.traininggreatminds.com

My gratitude to Melissa Tiers at the Center for Integrative Hypnosis for her permission to include the bilateral stimulation and peripheral vision techniques from her *Anti-Anxiety Toolkit*.

www.melissatiers.com

Useful Organisations

Anxiety UK: www.anxiety.co.uk
Email: info@anxietyuk.org.uk

CBT Register UK – Cognitive Behavioural and
Rational Emotive Behavioural Therapists
www.cbtregisteruk.com

General Hypnotherapy Register
www.generalhypnotherapyregister.com

MIND: www.mind.org.uk
Email: contact@mind.org.uk

YoungMinds: www.youngminds.org.uk
Email: ymenquiries@youngminds.org.uk

General Hypnotherapy Register
www.generalhypnotherapyregister.com

References and Resources

Articles

Buxton, O. M., cited by Hadhazy A., in 'Why does the sound of Water Help you Sleep?' www.livescience.com. 18 January 2016,

Gould van Praag, C., et al. (2017) It's True. The sound of nature helps us relax. Science Daily, 30 March 2017.

Partington, P., (2017) Guided Visualisation, Cognitive Defusion Techniques, The Plastic Brain, adapted from Anxiety. A User's Manual for the Brain

Shuster, R., cited in How the Beach benefits your Brain, According to Science, Gherini, A., Inc.com, 2017

Books

Jennifer Kavanagh, Heart of Oneness, A little book of connection, Christian Alternative Books, 2017

Ella Woodward, Deliciously Ella, Yellow Kite, 2015

Further suggested reading:

David Burns, When Panic Attacks, Harmony, 2006

Matt Haig, Notes on a Nervous Planet, Penguin, 2018

Avy Joseph and Maggie Chapman, Visual CBT, Capstone, 2013

Erling Kagge, Silence in the Age of Noise, Random House, 2017

Alastair McIntosh, Schumacher Briefings, Rekindling Community, Connecting People, Environment and Spirituality, (15) Green Books, 2008

Emma Mitchell, Michael O'Mara, The Wild Remedy, How Nature Mends Us, 2018

For information on foods that may help with Anxiety and Stress, see:

www.psycom.net – 8 Foods That Help with Anxiety and Stress.

www.ncbi.nlm.nih.gov/pubmed/25998000

www.highernature.com

For further resources/worksheets:

www.getselfhelp.co.uk

"When it gets dark enough, you can see the stars"

Lee Salk – child psychologist and author

Lightning Source UK Ltd.
Milton Keynes UK
UKHW012026240222
399195UK00001B/15